# FLYING GECKO

## The Flying Gecko Is A Nocturnal Reptile So It Requires Only One Light Bulb

By O.D JOE

# Table of Contents

## CHAPTER ONE

# A FLYING GECKO CARE SHEET

The flying gecko, also known as the gliding gecko or parachute gecko, is a small, quirky, and fascinating creature. The spry little reptile is called the flying gecko and has names related to flying because of its amazing ability to glide from tree to tree in the wild tropical rainforests of Southeast Asia.

The flying geckos are not your common pets but these beautiful creatures have become relatively popular pets amongst the reptile lovers' community.

### Quick Reference Section

- **Experience level:** Intermediate to Experienced
- **Family:** Gekkonidae
- **Scientific name:** Gekko Kuhli
- **Other Names:** Kuhl's Flying Gecko, Gliding gecko, Kuhl's Parachute Gecko
- **Average adult size:** 4-8 inches
- **Lifespan:** 5-8 years
- **Clutch Size:** 1-2 eggs
- **Egg Incubation Period:** 60-90 days
- **Food:** Variety of insects, crickets, and worms
- **Average Temperature:** 90°H/70°L
- **Humidity:** 60-80%
- **UVB lighting:** optional
- **Average price range:** $20 – $40
- **Conservation Status:** "Least Concern"

## Flying Gecko Facts

The Flying Gecko or Gliding Gecko (Scientific-Gekko Kuhli) is a unique, skittish, and timid reptile. It belongs to the Family Gekkonidae and Genus Gekko.

These little critters are native to Southeast Asian tropical rainforests, mostly coming from the Malaysian Peninsula, Indonesia, Thailand, Sumatra, and other surrounding areas and countries.

These little geckos' main colors are generally brown with darker brown or black speckles, and their underbellies are usually lighter with a beige tone. Patterns vary greatly from lizard to lizard.

These little tree-dwellers are incredibly camouflaged and can blend in with their habitats. This trait helps them avoid predators.

The exact size varies. More often, flying geckos grow to about 4 to 8 inches from tongue to tail tip. And, these geckos feature prominent skin flaps along their sides, tails, and feet. These flaps help them camouflage and enable them to glide through their tropical environments.

Other than the flaps, the webbed feet, and flattened tail help and allow them to glide around. Like many other gecko species, the flying geckos have microscopic hairs on their toes that can adhere to most surfaces, including glass.

## Flying Gecko Habitat

### *Enclosure*

It is not recommended to give your flying gecko room to glide unless you can provide a large natural outdoor enclosure, because they have been observed to hurt themselves by gliding into thc walls of thc enclosure.

For an adult flying gecko, a 15-gallon tank is the minimum size recommended, though you can give them a bit more. Exo Terra makes a good one. For two geckos, a 20-gallon would be an adequate size if you plan for some romantic breeding time.
Don't put two males in an enclosure together.

One more thing to keep in mind when looking for an enclosure is, height is more important than length because they tend to spend little time on the ground.

Make sure they have plenty of places to climb since these critters love to spend most of their time above the ground. Provide fairly dense foliage throughout the cage.

Either live or fake plants will do and other things like rocks can be added to decorate. Make sure you have a sufficient amount of hiding spots around the enclosure's foliage. Clean regularly, mist the cage twice a day, and spot clean as needed.

### *Substrate*

Because of humidity requirements, the absorbent substrate is recommended. The substrate can simply be layers of paper towels, though peat moss or coconut fiber is most preferred.

More natural substrates like non-fertilized potting soil will also do. Replace substrate when needed. For options, check out Zoo Med Repti Bark. It lasts up to one year before you'd need to replace it.

### *Temperature*

As with many reptiles, there should be a basking spot on one end of the enclosure and a cool side as well. The basking spot should be kept around 90 degrees and the cool side of the enclosure should range from 70-80 degrees. Some recommend using OMAYKEY Ceramic Heat Lamp.

### *Humidity*

Flying Geckos require high humidity. Something like the BaoGuai Reptile Mister should suffice.
Spray the enclosure twice daily with a spray bottle. Spray until the enclosure and decorations are dripping.

Keep it so because when thirsty, the gecko will drink the water droplets from the leaves and decorations. Humidity levels should be kept between 60%-80%.

### *Lighting*

The flying gecko is a nocturnal reptile so it requires only one light bulb. There is no current study that suggests that this lizard requires UVB lighting.

Some reptile owners, however, prefer to provide UVB. Something such as the Evergreen UVA/UVB Mercury Vapor Bulb may be an option.

CHATTER TWO

# FLYING GECKO FEEDING

Like most small reptiles, flying geckos are insectivores. Their diets consist mainly of a variety of crickets, and worms such as earthworms, mealworms, waxworms, hornworms, silkworms, and redworms. On some occasions, they are known to accept feeding on nightcrawlers.

Adults should be fed about 15 insects every three or so days. Young geckos should be fed between 5-10 insects until they are full every day.

Make sure geckos are getting needed nutrients by dusting food items every week. Dust every other day for young hatchlings. Consider reptile multivitamins and calcium supplements like Vetark Nutrobal.
Place a small soaking dish for your flying gecko. Though the gecko will lick water droplets off of leaves when they get thirsty, the water dish is for soaking their skin in when they become too dry.

## Temperament

Like most small reptiles, flying geckos are insectivores. Their diets consist mainly of a variety of crickets, and worms such as earthworms, mealworms, waxworms, hornworms, silkworms, and redworms.

On some occasions, they are known to accept feeding on nightcrawlers.

Adults should be fed about 15 insects every three or so days. Young geckos should be fed between 5-10 insects until they are full every day.

Make sure geckos are getting needed nutrients by dusting food items every week. Dust every other day for young hatchlings. Consider reptile multivitamins and calcium supplements like Vetark Nutrobal.
Place a small soaking dish for your flying gecko. Though the gecko will lick water droplets off of leaves when they get thirsty, the water dish is for soaking their skin in when they become too dry.

### Temperament

Like most small reptiles, flying geckos are insectivores. Their diets consist mainly of a variety of crickets, and worms such as earthworms, mealworms, waxworms, hornworms, silkworms, and redworms.
On some occasions, they are known to accept feeding on nightcrawlers.

Adults should be fed about 15 insects every three or so days. Young geckos should be fed between 5-10 insects until they are full every day.

Make sure geckos are getting needed nutrients by dusting food items every week. Dust every other day for young hatchlings. Consider reptile multivitamins and calcium supplements like Vetark Nutrobal.
Place a small soaking dish for your flying gecko. Though the gecko will lick water droplets off of leaves when they get thirsty, the water dish is for soaking their skin in when they become too dry.

## Temperament

## Conclusion

For a beginner, caring for a flying gecko is not suggested. But if a said novice is an attentive owner up for a challenge, then you can give these exotic creatures a go.

These geckos don't need much stimulation but make sure you have the right habitat for them, and you are all good to go.

The flying gecko is one exotic, majestic, and interesting little reptile. Though they are not quite affectionate and shy, they make for a really good display pet reptile.

CHAPTER THREE

# SPECIES SUMMARY

The flying gecko (*Ptychozoon Kohli*) is a unique little reptile that you don't see very often in the pet trade. They are one of the rarer gecko species, making them highly sought-after by serious herp-lovers.

These lizards are native to the jungles of Southeast Asia. But finding them is easier said than done! Flying geckos are masters of camouflage. Not only that, but they are arboreal and spend most of their life in the treetops!

**Despite their colorful name, these reptiles don't really "fly" at all.** Instead, they leap from one branch to the next. Thanks to their excess skin flaps, they can control their trajectory and glide to safety!

Of course, flying geckos aren't going to be doing much of that in captivity. However, you still need to provide a similar environment that caters to their unique lifestyle.

**Appearance & Colors**

Flying geckos have a muted appearance. Generally, they're covered in splotches of brown, black, and tan. The coloration is sporadic, giving it a natural appearance.

From afar, these lizards look like a piece of tree bark! They use their appearance to their advantage and blend in with trees in the wild.

You'll notice that flying geckos also have several flaps of skin on their body. These flaps are visible around the arms, tail, and face. Even the feet are webbed!

**As mentioned earlier, these flaps help the gecko control its movement in the air. The tail provides some stability as well. Its tail is flattened, allowing them to use it as a rudder. While they may seem a bit funky when these reptiles are on the ground, they look fantastic when being used in the air! Lifespan**

**The typical lifespan of a flying gecko is between five and eight years when kept in captivity.** However, that's only if you're providing top-notch care.

Like any other reptile, flying geckos can respond negatively to poor living conditions. You have to create a fine-tuned habitat to keep these critters healthy. Otherwise, they can suffer from disease and potentially an early death.

## Average Size

**The average size of a flying gecko is about four to eight inches in length for adults.** That makes these reptiles quite small when compared to other species.

The tail of this gecko isn't as long as you might expect. Not only that, but they often keep it curled up. When you combine this with their already wide appearance, these geckos often look rather short.

## CHAPTER FOUR

# FLYING GECKO CARE

Flying gecko care is a task that's best suited for herp-lovers with a bit of experience. While not particularly difficult to care for, these reptiles do have some distinct needs to thrive.

As an arboreal species, you have to go to greater lengths to ensure that their environment is conducive to their lifestyle. Here are some important care guidelines you need to follow.

### Enclosure Size

First things first, you need to choose the right enclosure! Many reptile enthusiasts will keep these geckos in standard terrariums. While that can work fine, **we always recommend using a vivarium-style enclosure.**

The reason for this is that vivariums have front-facing glass doors and adjustable ventilation, which can help create the perfect environment.

For single adult flying geckos, use an enclosure that's at least 12 inches long, 12 inches wide, and 24 inches tall. If you're using a standard terrarium, that would be about 15 to 20 gallons.

Height is the crucial measurement here. These geckos do not spend a ton of time on the ground (it's not where they feel safe), so you need ample height to accommodate climbing.

**Habitat Setup**

Establishing a proper habitat setup is always important when housing reptiles. But with a flying gecko, the decorations you use will have a big impact on the lizard's well-being!

To replicate their natural habitat, **fill the enclosure with climbable branches and vines.** To keep things low-maintenance, utilize plastic and silk plants.

Just because flying geckos are primarily arboreal doesn't mean you can neglect the other parts of the enclosure. Choose a simple substrate material for the bottom.

Some owners even use paper towels to keep your maintenance tasks easier, but coconut coir, peat moss, and fertilizer-free potting soil work well too.

Once you have your climbing branches set up, add some additional plants throughout the enclosure. The plants will provide some shelter and give these pet lizards places to hide. Traditional hide boxes at ground level are not necessary since flying geckos won't be spending time on the ground anyway.

However, **we recommend installing several perches and elevated hides around the enclosure.** Taller plants with ample foliage do the trick too!

CHATTER FIVE

# TEMPERATURE & LIGHTING

While they spend a ton of time high off the ground, flying geckos still need a temperature gradient in their habitat.

To create your gradient, you can use a basking lamp or heat emitter. **The basking lamp should warm up one side of the enclosure to about 95 degrees Fahrenheit.** Make sure the lamp is not too close to the case or any of the climbing branches.

**The rest of the enclosure can remain at room temperature.** Just make sure that temperatures don't dip below 76 degrees. If they do, you might need to install an under-tank heating pad or emitter.

## Humidity

Proper humidity levels are a must for any jungle-dwelling reptile. Invest in a high-quality hygrometer and check it regularly to ensure that levels are just right.

**Flying geckos prefer steady humidity levels of around 80 percent at night.** During the day, the humidity can drop to 60 percent, but no lower.

Mist the enclosure every night to raise the levels just before your gecko becomes active. You can also install an automatic mister or drip system if you wish.

## Water

Flying geckos do not drink water from bowls or dishes. Instead, they will lap droplets off plant leaves and the glass of the enclosure (which makes sense since they spend so much time in the trees).

**That said, it's still good to have a small water dish in their home.** They may use it to soak or cool off on occasion

We recommend installing a shallow soaking dish at the bottom of the enclosure. Another more elaborate option is to opt for an elevated dish that secures the glass.

Either way, make sure the dish is always clean and filled with fresh water.

## Food & Diet

Insects are the food of choice for flying geckos. In the wild, they hunt a wide range of different insects to meet their nutritional needs. In captivity, they do just fine with crickets, roaches, mealworms, waxworms, and sliced earthworms.

**A variety of food sources is always welcome.** Make sure that the insects are no bigger than the width of the gecko's head!

Young flying geckos will need to eat every day until they are full. Typically, this will be around five to 10 insects. Adults do best with large meals every two or three days. They may need up to 15 insects for each feeding.

## Possible Health Issues

Flying geckos are susceptible to all of the usual health conditions that geckos and other reptiles encounter in captivity.

**Some of the most common ailments are respiratory infections, bacterial infections, and parasites.** Most of these issues are avoidable with proper tank maintenance.

Stay on top of humidity and temperature levels to avoid respiratory infections. This should be rather easy if you have an accurate hygrometer.

To ensure that your lizard is living in a hygienic environment, spot clean the enclosure daily. Then, do a full sanitization about once a month. This involves cleaning every surface with a reptile-safe disinfectant.

Flying geckos can also suffer from physical injuries. They have very sensitive skin, so cuts are common. Do your best to remove any sharp or rough surfaces in the enclosure to prevent this from becoming a problem.

## Behavior & Temperament

Don't expect to see much of your flying gecko throughout the day! Most will find a cozy hiding spot to sleep in until the sun goes down.

At night, these creatures are quite active. They'll move from branch to branch as they explore and regulate their temperature.

Flying geckos can cohabitate with others, but you need to plan your group accordingly. One male and two females or a group of all females are best.

Males get very territorial with one another and will fight constantly. You should never house two males together. It's also a good idea to avoid housing larger geckos with smaller ones. Geckos that are the same age and size are best.

CHAPTER SIX

# HANDLING TIPS

Flying geckos are not pet reptiles that you want to handle. There are a couple of reasons for this:

First, these reptiles are far too timid for handling. The moment you try to grab them, they will flee!

Even if you're lucky enough to get ahold of one, it will do everything it can to jump from your hand and get away from you. It's just their nature! They don't like being handled at all.

Another reason to avoid handling flying geckos is their skin. The reptiles have very thin skin that will easily tear. It doesn't take much to injure these lizards, so they're best enjoyed from the other side of a glass enclosure.

We think this reptile is unique enough that you can get plenty of enjoyment from observing them. However, if you're adamant about getting a pet you can handle frequently, this isn't the one for you.

## Conclusion

Even though these lizards are a bit out of the ordinary, they're fairly simple to keep. While we don't recommend them for beginners, owners with a little bit of experience shouldn't have trouble meeting the care requirements of a flying gecko

And trust us, it's worth it! These reptiles are extremely rewarding to keep, and even more fun to observe. You'll find yourself pushing back your bedtime just to squeeze in some extra time watching them!

Let us know if you still have questions after reading this care sheet. We know flying geckos are a little unusual, so there's plenty to consider!

THE END

www.ingramcontent.com/pod-product-compliance
Lightning Source LLC
LaVergne TN
LVHW052117160826
845678LV00015B/3592

* 9 7 9 8 3 5 1 7 1 0 9 5 2 *